THE CHIMNEY STONE

T0151325

 NIGHTWOOD EDITIONS

2010 ∾ Gibsons, BC

NIGHTWOOD EDITIONS

2010

The Chimney Stone

ROB WINGER

Ghazals

Nightwood Editions
P.O. Box 1779
Gibsons, BC V0N 1V0
Canada
www.nightwoodeditions.com

THE CANADA COUNCIL | LE CONSEIL DES ARTS
FOR THE ARTS | DU CANADA
SINCE 1957 | DEPUIS 1957

BRITISH
COLUMBIA
ARTS COUNCIL
Supported by the Province of British Columbia

Nightwood Editions acknowledges financial support from the Government of
Canada through the Canada Book Fund and the Canada Council for the Arts,
and from the Province of British Columbia through the British Columbia Arts
Council and the Book Publisher's Tax Credit.

This book has been produced on 100% post-consumer recycled, ancient-forest-
free paper, processed chlorine-free and printed with vegetable-based dyes.

TYPESETTING & COVER DESIGN: Carleton Wilson

Printed and bound in Canada

LIBRARY AND ARCHIVES CANADA CATALOGUING IN PUBLICATION

Winger, Robert, 1974-
     The chimney stone / Rob Winger.

Poems.
ISBN 978-0-88971-249-2

     I. Title.

PS8645.I573C55 2010   C811'.6   C2010-904364-2

∾

*once
again:*

*for Kristal
and our
Davis*

∾

Contents

III. Idiot Wind

IV. Blind Date

GHAZAL FOR TUNING YOUR MALACHI

Listen: of course they don't care about poems,
about your hunting knife.

The dykes hold, and birds. *Water, water everywhere,*
and not a drop to drink;

the tides could sure as hell care
less about us.

He wouldn't shut up because you asked him to;
mud so thick we can't get our ears off the cornstalks.

Along High Marsh trails: rose of Sharon, broken bridge.
In Slack's Cove: a nineteenth-century cairn.

Ropes on Hart Hall. Corner floorboards. The shot clock, and Tobin.
The office you left, filled with theory.

Time to split wood, dive deep, surface
at the edge of the chopping.

Here's to Polaris and goalposts, gravestones, narcissus;
here's to a final line that's the dawn.

(When the fire's done,
 who holds onto ashes?)

I

Iron John

Sometimes I think the stars scrape at my door, wanting in;
I'm watching the hockey game

~ John Thompson

Ghazal for Cash

Dammit, John, *I'm trying to write a poem*, here. Your June, your Hurt;
six decades on the hard disk. Bass E. No books.

The thesaurus as species, as fossil. *Pure memory.*
A tumour the size of a football, cut.

My grandfather's knife. Cut glass, scored,
then shattered in a metal barrel;

in the sunroom, his wife crushes wasps
with her thumb.

A gillnet's limit and your father's meshed blood;
the surface is a breached purgatory.

Are there enough stones cast in this river to jump across?
I've pulled a muscle.

GHAZAL FOR JARI KURRI

He and I see the game the same way:
the same source, the same lust, the same surgery his mind was capable of.

Finnish sandwich, Flash, the Great One;
at the centre of our lives: this naming.

Carbon and monoxide: the old Detroit perfume.
Everybody take a whiff, on me.

Your best bet's an accidental trifecta: rye, clever, jackdaw;
there's no such thing as synonyms.

It's too late to catch Carter's homer, Hokusai's Fuji, Apollo's thrusters;
why wait for the right Winger to pass?

GHAZAL FOR TWO LULLABIES

The water's wide, but where's the ferry?
Give me a boat that will carry two.

We can do without kitchens and fire.
I'll cut a hole and pull you through.

Our son on the hearthstone, a jumping jack.
Our faces corked for a Fisk Jubilee.

My back's bark bow'd, and syne it brak.
If swung low, where could they carry me?

Open the woodshed and look at the stain.
If I cross over, will we put to sea?

If I do, what then, iron red, Iron John?
Your lines cast deep, as deep can be.

Ghazal for Harmony Road

We rise from marinas into melodrama.
On the counter, the Macallan's half-full.

I want to write war novels and drink, sucker-punch the busboy;
which bits of men are worth applause?

Out of ditches, the road rises. Fault lines swell. I lose
my footing;

so give me *Alligator Pie*, teddy-bear pancakes, an angry branch ticking
the nightmare's window.

Should I *climb right out of the machinery*, or dig
in, web, build me some good, frosted fences?

Rich, we'd buy the house on the hill and grow pumpkins;
how many children have we lost to friction?

Pause the traffic and cardinals will come to your feeder;
smeared sand in a shattered mandala.

When the road ends, we'll plunge
into gravel, find

the old man in the young child,
the alchemist in the engineer.

The bulb needs a vacuum to burn, buddy.
Is this the dark you've been looking for?

GHAZAL FOR PAS

Eadweard's dead. He's dead.
Chuck another lump on the fire, Scrooge.

The moon rose for you, too. I know that.
We've lost your bread crumbs in the undergrowth.

That's not it. River; spring weed;
not the fossils.

It's not Yasgur's farm we're after;
we've got to get ourselves back to the garden.

On the screen: bombs in Algiers, that torso torque;
each suitcase holds a thousand pixels.

(The difference between a sign and a song is
an I.)

Who's anxious? John's dead as a doornail, isn't he?
Why am I paging *apophrades*?

Turn the band-saw teeth into your thumb.
I'll keep piling blood.

Pearl, what are you waiting for, blinking that eye?
A burning thing, your cursor.

Ghazal for MacGowan's Molars

At fifty, you find the orthodontist's drills and caps;
all that you can remember now: little kids without no shoes.

Ice, missed stair, traffic;
is every infant just a pink slip?

Below forty metres
oxygen goes toxic in the cylinder.

Romeo, are you still below that balustrade in your peacock-blue beret?
Is this the East, or what?

The guard rail braces, then bursts;
escarpment cedar pulled from the earth, by fenders.

After an eerie rain, you can't swim. The snows of Kilimanjaro?
The glacier's gone and the plane's delayed.

Is New York still some fairy tale,
some old bum in the same old drunk tank?

And *if the rivers all run dry,* Shane,
what about the currents?

GHAZAL FOR FINGERISM

for Don

You map the sidewalk into chickadees;
these cars, this cement, and still that mating call, that chorus.

The fog and your concept of fog;
by the 7-Eleven could be Milarepa, a flyby Slurpee.

You've got the moon, and your memory of moons;
read after hours, with bulbs.

Mongrels by the kitchen want rice, so an orange monk stoops to earth;
accuracy: the stone he throws digging a dog's ribs.

In the newspaper are blood rivers, Lhasa and fire: choose your decade;
repair those cellular clock gears.

The beach beads against chrome, chum.
If an ocean answers, ready won't matter.

GHAZAL FOR THE *BLONDE ON BLONDE* BLUES

Newport, and we electrify placards:
why bother to hurl tomatoes?

Pitches get redirected, don't they?
On the sidewalk, toddlers zip towards pickups.

Woody, you're gone, so I'll paint you a hospital, get me some
good car to drive, after a war.

Half a wine bottle later, the structured professor explodes:
sometimes I might get drunk, walk like a duck and smell like a skunk.

Trying to prove that your conclusions should be more drastic,
you slam the library door: go fuck yourself, Lacan.

Don't think twice, Bob;
there's blood on the tracks, all right.

Ghazal for Jackpine Dust

If they come with knives,
put your skull into that tortoise shell.

In the library's dust, someone's carved a cartoon cock;
as good as any reason.

The auction paddle falls against your wallet;
at the podium: Tom Thomson's cadmium, sold to bankers.

Nixon gives up the ghost. Those V'd fingers, airborne.
Patpong's sisters stolen for GI Joe.

When the waves arrive, you lay down
and let them.

Our dusky park is surrounded by bodies;
at the bottom of the slide: dust and ashes.

Anti-Ghazal for the Met's Tanka

Behind glass are legs, an elbow, inked, that means
breakage, that tells us your arm changed, descending

to your belly, so its sable length is minutes,
black freckles, maybe, on an eager, Honshu smock.

The etched tree is a cherry blossom front, signed;
the bamboo ribs that line its lantern, and this   drop

that's a signal for light, the combed stones of gardens,
what's left when syllables shift to pictogram.

In each of the parchment's pocks: full hours;
my wide sweep of ocean behind your bloody brush.

GHAZAL FOR *THE STAIRCASE LETTERS*
for Arthur

Purple violet cuts your legs, running to Silver Lake, 1972;
there are six houses between you, now. And blood.

Letters spill from novels;
on the answering machine could be Yeats, Hopkins.

My grandfather's spiles tap trunks;
the neighbour's bucket (filled with dirt).

The lawnmower's so loud you're mute. My narrow poems
and your wide white beam, walking yard: *Spem reduxit.*

So many people have died already,
what's the point?

On the beach: the hunter. Grand designs as insect wings
and all our denouements.

GHAZAL FOR HELL'S MORNING

An ocean is god's bedspread;
if the surface is a gale, the depths don't know it.

Arthur, Vincent, John, Ghalib: are you listening? It's Morning.
Slaves, let us not curse life.

This morning there are maggots in the pantry;
I crush them with a bleached paper towel.

Yeah, it's true: we drink and the bombs keep falling;
every guidance system: a failed proof.

Under the hijab you find follicles, not fuses.
Poison on the neighbour's lawn. The water table, spent.

Luck is your newborn feasting on a backyard riot of dogshit;
watch where you step, Winger; none of them ever meant it.

II

Bloody Mary

there won't be a mention in the news of the world
about the life and the death of a red dirt girl

∽ Emmylou Harris

GHAZAL AGAINST THE WASP'S NEST

You whine about the rip in your Cadillac's leather. Me,
about being born in the Cadillac.

Where, in my body, are the first molecules of gentleness?
Cheering the fourth line, late, in the third.

And why perceive a town, standing?
The women, beaten; their sons' fists, by example.

There's no Song of Solomon: he won't walk the ocean floor.
Why have I inherited these struts?

Flowers in snow, love in the Rockies:
spare me your sugar and light.

Giving up isn't enough, not guilt, not heated lecterns;
in the Congo, they're still slicing lips in two with steel.

A heart of darkness is still a heart;
there's no excuse, past the barred gate, for letting it stay up.

GHAZAL FOR ANOTHER HERE

How can your busted, angry heart be Ontario?
That red country truck was my grandfather's Bible.

Your skin's no accident;
a shovel and rose, a breached levy. Elmina.

Your psychoanalysis has forgotten
its mirror.

A flame don't always need no match
to burn.

There are Soviets in the space heater;
put down your rifle and write.

GHAZAL AGAINST MUZZLES

At the bar: cowboy heels on the railing, bullshit belts;
we're folding bills against her waistline.

Tourists in Auschwitz, Dresden: *ready*
for the laughing gas;

how many does it take to screw in, to figure, to solve?
No matter your math, our money will never love mothers.

The sea's no garden, sweetheart;
nature's not Eden.

Give it a rest, boy; *let there*
be light.

GHAZAL FOR THE WATER GLASS

for K.

Admit it: there's *Annie Hall*, *Casablanca*, Harry at the Met's pyramid;
there's *Astral Weeks*, *Pink Moon*, cheap pretzels, baseball.

And, oh, *pphhew!*, that beach, that shore. Asleep, and full.
That self-same saccharine sky continued. Light and light. No photos.

The greybeards break: wind and undertow;
a careful line of sand beneath evergreens: Toni Morrison's locks.

We are tent, yurt, cabin; we are pine-soft truss, bamboo hut, duvet;
your grandfather plants a poplar windbreak long before you're born.

Our red wall bench: Toksu lunch, a clean drift of cherry trees,
same ankles. Stride, and stride, and stride.

My granddad's band saw, your father's peg leg: corpus callosum;
newspapers a foot deep in the corner.

Showers in Phuket, Kamala, McLeod Ganj; that high tide, Samet.
Who draws straws for oceans?

If you swaddle the crib's nightmare,
is my *tick tick tick* the sure quilt's bark?

GHAZAL AGAINST THE LAST STRAW

you keep on falling, cause there ain't no bottom.
✍ Emmylou Harris

Are your teeth angry or injured?
What's the point of asking?

I see your bags packed and ready on the busted sidewalk;
the only sure shelter is children.

What happens when we take the iambs away
from the bank cages?

Sometimes the codes won't scan.
If you want me, I'll be in the bar.

Can I admit the strides of women?
Last page, first tremor, harvest.

I watch your ankle climb the temple to an aspara's lipstick;
is this the great leap forward?

The point is a spit
of land.

When your rooster crows at the break of dawn, look out your window, love:
the future of nostalgia is utopia.

GHAZAL FOR BLANKS

Blue roots in your wrist:
a clever blade cuts Act IV.

Body found (in the river in the concrete in the trench in the mouth):
all dropped bulbs mean spring.

The moraine's slope cuts
hydro lines.

You punch down the bread, its glass bowl;
if your jump lands in the kitchen...

Roses and bronze and white candles and moon;
the careful condom breaks.

This fade-out into wheels is an engine block melting;
our compact Ford still coasting Ontario's concessions.

GHAZAL AGAINST PURE REASON

for Phyllis Webb

In your book, they've underlined, in pen,
all your lost allusions;

the metro costs
one pound.

Leave alone the dust in the courtyard;
rake the stones to think them broken.

New saplings, planted, in their concrete bowls;
a pot tips off the porch and spills bulbs onto bedrock.

In the next wave are Basho's long-lost verticals;
his kanji legs: a split oak, six hundred years between us.

Is memory our only way forward?
The earth furrows its brow.

Pigs in a blanket, pimps in diamonds;
a dear birdie on the company bill.

Hydrangeas in the ditch, pigs in the shit;
in Jo'burg, you're born in a cradle of tin.

Beneath light: marine snow.
Forget eternity; the soup's heat means winter.

Where's your Rilke, Rob?
In the slow brush strokes behind Billie Holiday?

(Wait. Wait just a minute.)

This is no frog match;
there's only me.

III

Idiot Wind

the thing I came for:
the wreck and not the story of the wreck
the thing itself and not the myth

Adrienne Rich

GHAZAL FOR THE BIRTHDAY HOTEL

Why insist on records? Better build
an eavestrough, discover brick, sleep.

Let's get this straight: does setting the chimney stone
promise fire?

Ordered calendars and icing;
why shuck the grave's nightdress?

The ice buckles under a hot stream
in the urinal.

Takhallus; suit yourself;
get to the bloody point.

Listen, idiot wind, the body won't serve
until you forget it.

GHAZAL FOR EMPTY NETS

I'm tired of lyrics;
what else is there?

Give me a letter, a compass, a midnight shrimpboat.
Without footholds, the summit's limestone is maritime.

Hold, and hold the body, so your shudder breaks scales;
whip tip, your hot contact is a white dwarf.

If you light the fire,
bring books.

Decades past their plots: the floor plans of grandparent gardens;
why wrap presents in ribbon?

Are we all still lost in the same old
supermarket?

Wake up, buddy: you're dreaming. The walls are almost
syntax, almost the lost peonies of my circadia.

GHAZAL FOR SOLO RADIF (AS QAFIA)

Miles between us, so what else matters?: Col-
trane, *Bitch's Brew*, early Bird: birth control.

This morning we're cheesecloth around curds, blocked;
thick milk rots at the base of *Wilson's Bowl*.

Dusk: a vapour trail's smokescreen. Remember:
even off-grid organics still need coal.

Emmylou, Dixie, Dolly, Kate: god help
me through this gospel country, old brown souls.

Why can't lines be broken? Wake up, pal; meet
your maker, change the leading, pay the toll.

GHAZAL FOR LORATADINE

Suspend your adverbs;
the dictionary's bacterial.

If we raise our clubs, what will bring them
down again?

$C_{22}H_{23}CIN_2O_2$: dip into the bloodstream.
Bend the bone until it snaps.

Over the falls, your world's a cracker barrel;
will we dance the polka, or smash our ribs on the rocks?

Your digits punch keys; on the screen: blanks.
Sparrow skulls, crushed by car grills.

He films his monologue online, forearms glistening;
what else lets loose when his guns come out? (The college lintels?)

Your alphabet diphthongs, fuses, syllables.
At ten months, all of our prayers are *mama*.

GHAZAL FOR A FIELD PEARL

for Aaron

It's buried, friend; pay up and dig;
you're already a mile up your Bomunsan.

On the highway, you pull into a siding and flatten the pedal;
the time between planets is a smooth, deep ditch.

Pixies and femmes, rotted teeth, Ian Curtis;
backstage, your razor carves a sternum's arrow.

Refuse leather, cheese, *The Satanic Verses*, cookbooks;
put your finger in his rib cage, Thomas.

Blood and body, bread and wine:
save me, Aaron, from my lyric's lukewarm pews.

GHAZAL FOR THE NORDIK

Our kids know the sea can blanket, can be blank;
can roll over, embrace. Polyp.

The tap takes time; throats and elbows.
The sink means hope, u-bend, joint.

Snow as film/still, apex, doldrums;
snow as indecision; snow as grain.

Cold current, granite lip: a spine's pressure leaks salt.
The torrent between labels: what's possible and what's done.

In the trees are crystals, seeds; there could be angels.
I'm asleep.

GHAZAL FOR THE SWEETWATER SEA

Hey, *Chi-Cheemaun*: are you making these gull-hitching gusts,
or were they there already, forty feet above the blues?

Stick your face straight into the gale or it'll rip your glasses off;
if you wake up on deck, the world's a folded map.

Another yawned crossing, white Jesuits on the North Channel;
bread and wine and oil.

A body lost here is sucked into currents, so hold on;
fair wind, and plenty.

Poems, I don't want you:
there's no salt left on my old, white mountain.

Ghazal for Bang Krut

A fish hook tears into knuckle. Lines and lines and
lines tie you to the reef.

This is a storm, a spoon. No. This is a *st-*, a *sp-*.
No. The waves, metallic. No, *the waves* -   no.

Object: how creamy lines explode onto beaches, with meter.
That's it.

Every wall in this house is so white and air-conditioned,
there's no sun.

Blue paint regulator rib-cage fins:
we straddle air tanks in the swimming pool.

Longtail's orchids and the golden Theravada temple:
a postcard's beatified bureaucracy.

In memoirs, we put dead groupers on the beach:
salvage anthropology for tourists.

We descend along an anchor line. At the bottom, my guide
drifts into the brown zero. I'm tied, solo, to the rope.

Ghazal for Sheet Lightning

Unfold your glasses;
between nightstand and vision is the meaning of distance.

A birch's stormstruck bloodstream;
the bomb in the baby carriage, wired to the radio.

Think of your books, patchwork, the wild weight of laundry;
your attic mother at a kitchen window, yellow.

If there's an answer, so what?
The lightning's still three bays away.

The wall's blue fire and the hydro plant;
rake the coals. They're hot.

That I understand nothing is an understanding;
dew worms, leaves: terrible angels.

GHAZAL FOR FIRE

House it in a winter pot;
read your leaves.

In the ditch: a cleansing;
in the canopy: five hundred years make way for coffee.

Why bother with teepees, a schoolhouse?
If it's liquid, won't blue take over, anyhow?

I'll gather twigs, what's fallen; .
the wet bark still won't burn.

. None of us arrive without lamps, cords cut, iodine;
the concrete tiles are limestone ash.

If you burn, slash first;
the killdeers won't leave their nests.

IV

Blind Date

The proper response to a poem is another poem.

∽ Phyllis Webb

GHAZAL FOR GAZELLES

It's not what you write, but how; close your scripts and say it.
The wreck, but not its story; get to grips and say it.

Fallen in with thieves, your world becomes a beaten ditch;
for the Bible tells me so they resist and say it.

1959: you climb Annapurna's exile;
we'll hold your photo to our sutured lips and say it.

Fox, wolf, killer whale: why target your own lost children?
Is God just to his creatures? (Lose those whips and say it.)

After the argument, I'll get in the car and drive;
where the great plains begin, will coulees and quicksand say it?

In the blast zone, Lenin's forehead peels into mushrooms;
at the swimmer's moment, pal, scale the tips and say it.

GHAZAL FOR JUNE 4, 1989 (FAILED)

Step past the Imperial Garden and T-59s;
across the street, the square's washed clean with kites.

In the alley, kitchen, serrated politics enter
our daughters.

Lao Tzu, why are you writing governance?
The fish in the pond is a citizen of nowhere.

The first runway in Lhasa is roses and sand;
when the planes land, why bother to grow similes?

Please come out of the cupboards, kids. *See we ain't got no swing
except for the ring of that truncheon thing*

and the sign across the street has lost its bookends:
" om Hardware" it says. Red.

Ghazal for S-21 (Failed)

Robusta dirt and this non-recycled lid;
a bean in full sun means crop dust.

Before execution, one shot only is the rule. Meter on a temple,
setting greyscales.

Try to equate Hitler and you'll end up
diamonds.

Barefoot to the old classroom, iron bites her shackled calf;
why do we keep such pictures

and why the hell are we looking, seven portraits missing?
are *Swimming to...* or "Holiday in..." really enough for Duch?

At Preah Khan, banyan roots swallow the wall;
sunlight slipping over stone, just like sunlight.

Ghazal for Newtons: May 10, 1748

When the mainmast snaps, seven sisters watch you sink;
before this, the world had no equator.

Put your coals back
in the chimney.

Why not build the bricks as tall as you can?
If the floorboards sound, they do.

Here's your faith's review and expectation, tied to the naval grating;
one lash for every thousand in the hold.

If you reach for the middle,
every edge is an apple.

At the bottom of the well, there's water.
How do you get from there to the pole star?

Crystal cave dendrites, fan corals,
are you still bright without us?

Leave the Christmas tree alone;
its needles want fire.

At the cash, we choose between *Combat Rock*
and *Thriller*;

Shareef don't like it, boys.
I guess we better let that raga drop.

GHAZAL FOR DECEMBER 9, 1964

John, teach me your counterpoint to Jimmy Garrison:
your *Om*; your *Train*.

The glass between clouds means pressure;
driver's-side blade, busted all winter.

Phrase and phrase and phrase and phrase:
one note for each hymn's syllabus.

The water splits around rock;
who built this bridge across the current?

When you die at forty, I'm unborn;
stack of old calendars in the blue box.

GHAZAL FOR ONCE IN A LIFETIME

Look *under the rocks and stones:*
there is water at the bottom of the ocean.

Not my beautiful house, then, *my wife*.
Carve your name into trees and their barks will fill you in.

Here a twister comes; here comes the twister.
Please put up your arm.

Time is a holding up, a current;
time means the water holds, a damning.

Into the blue, the red, *the silent water;*
two fingers, a half-pint, pipe: *same as it ever was*.

Why ask where the highway goes to?
Now that the money's gone, you'll find fingers in your pocket.

GHAZAL FOR ONCE IN A LIFETIME, II

First ice crystals on the pond's skin, again.
Why this constant need to begin, again?

The funeral's over, your prints on the screen.
Dixie Chicks: rein that landslide in again.

In another part of the world, next time,
we'll push: fists, bed, your neck, your skin, again.

Huck, why're we still living in that *shotgun
shack*? Can't we do the same for Jim again?

Water dissolving and water removing;
current in a valley of springs again.

Son, you're lifted above the C-section:
I'll snip your blue braid. A wake: Finnegan.

GHAZAL FOR KING MOUNTAIN TRAIL

Eardley, here's where your basement split and your scars rose;
a shell that inverts your stomach, relaunched in the Sunday skull.

Cardinal, porcupine, Lorne Greene, bread crumbs:
that any of us survive makes calculus comedy.

Put the blade to your creamy throat;
navigate.

On the mountain, a fossilized star pushes
against its lost ocean.

Not what your shotgun meant, then, but how it was cocked;
the bullet's barrel is a depth charge.

Black swallower, anglerfish, tripod:
above the abyssal, you're monsters.

GHAZAL FOR KING-SIZE BELVEDERES, 1974

You build your darkroom, press, and the pond watches;
his old foundation, rotten; and his grave.

Blue cigarette box in the John Thompson fonds: *the user is*
the content of the poems.

Boy's strangled sky, white walls, cobblestones:
the spinning top he picks up shatters five new ribs.

Powder, syringe, love drug, diamond;
in the village square, someone's firstborn carves his father's trachea.

Tree-bark tea, red and read;
we import everything you can't spell.

Panting Bangkok apartment window:
hungry dogs and the one circled female.

Hang on, son: forget the landing net;
we'll dip our hooks in the stream and pull out bread.

NOTES

Quoted material frequently appears in italics throughout the poems.

Main epigraphs are taken from Phyllis Webb's *Hanging Fire* (Talonbooks: 1990), Adrienne Rich's "Diving into the Wreck" (Norton: 1973), and John Thompson's *Stilt Jack* (Anansi: 1978). Epigraphs for both "Bloody Mary" and "Ghazal for the Last Straw" are from Emmylou Harris' song and album, *Red Dirt Girl* (Nonesuch Records: 2000).

"Ghazal for Tuning Your Malachi" includes a common misquote of Samuel Taylor Coleridge's "The Rime of the Ancient Mariner"; it also names John Thompson's first book, *At the Edge of the Chopping There Are No Secrets* (Anansi: 1973); "Ghazal for the Birthday Hotel" quotes Ghazal XXX's final couplet in Thompson's *Stilt Jack*; and the line "the user is / the content of the poems" in "Ghazal for King-Size Belvederes, 1974" is written (in Thompson's hand) on a cigarette pack preserved at National Library and Archives Canada.

"Ghazal for Cash" refers to a cover of "Hurt" (written by Trent Reznor) on Johnny Cash's *American Recordings IV* (Universal: 2002). The "burning thing" in "Ghazal for Pas" comes from "Ring of Fire" (1963), co-written by Cash with June Carter.

The phrase *"pure memory"* in "Ghazal for Cash" is from Christopher Dewdney's *A Palaeozoic Geology of London, Ontario* (Coach House: 1974); *"I am trying to write a poem"* comes from Phyllis Webb's *Naked Poems* (Periwinkle: 1965). Another Webb title, *Wilson's Bowl* (Coach House: 1980), appears in "Ghazal for Solo Radif (as Qafia)."

"Ghazal for Jari Kurri" quotes Wayne Gretzky and Michael Ondaatje, respectively, the first in an undated interview, the second in *Coming Through Slaughter* (Anansi: 1976); it also names the American folk tune, "Take a Whiff on Me," and borrows from "Papa Hobo" on *Paul Simon* (Columbia: 1972). The fourth line of "Ghazal for Sheet Lightning" alters lyrics from "The Boy in the Bubble" on Simon's *Graceland* (Warner Bros.: 1986).

"Ghazal for Two Lullabies" combines lyrics from "The Water Is Wide" and "Swing Low, Sweet Chariot."

"Ghazal for Harmony Road" quotes Peter Gabriel's "Solsbury Hill" (Atco/Charisma: 1977), Dennis Lee's *Alligator Pie* (Macmillan: 1974), and Gaston Bachelard's *The Psychoanalysis of Fire* (1938; English translation: Beacon, 1964).

Lyrics by Joni Mitchell appear in "Ghazal against the Last Straw" and "Ghazal for Pas," the former borrowing a line from "A Case of You" on *Blue* (Reprise: 1971), and the latter quoting "Woodstock" on *Ladies of the Canyon* (Reprise: 1970). "Ghazal for Pas" also refers to Al Purdy's *Piling Blood* (McClelland & Stewart: 1984).

"Ghazal for MacGowan's Molars" borrows lines from several Pogues' songs, including "The Sunnyside of the Street" on *Hell's Ditch* (Island: 1990) and both "Fairytale of New York" and "If I Should Fall from Grace with God" on *If I Should Fall from Grace with God* (Island: 1988).

"Ghazal for Fingerism" is partly based on Don Domanski's essay, "Poetry and the Sacred" (Vancouver Island U: Institute of Coastal Research, 2006).

"Ghazal for the *Blonde on Blonde* Blues" borrows titles and lyrics from Bob Dylan, including "Don't Think Twice, It's All Right" (also quoted in "Ghazal for the Last Straw"), "Talkin' World War III Blues," and "I Shall Be Free" from *The Freewheelin' Bob Dylan* (Columbia: 1963); the albums *Blonde on Blonde* (Columbia: 1966) and *Blood on the Tracks* (Columbia: 1975); and "Queen Jane Approximately" from *Highway 61 Revisited* (Columbia: 1965). Dylan's "Idiot Wind" (from *Blood on the Tracks*) provides the title for section three and also appears in the final couplet of "Ghazal for the Birthday Hotel."

"Ghazal for *The Staircase Letters*" refers to Arthur Motyer's book *The Staircase Letters* (Random House: 2007).

The second couplet of "Ghazal for Hell's Morning" translates a line from Arthur Rimbaud's "Morning" in *A Season in Hell*: "Esclaves, ne maudissons pas la vie."

Images, slave castles, and the red country truck in "Ghazal for Another Here" respond in part to Dionne Brand's books, especially *In Another Place, Not Here* (Knopf: 1996), *Land to Light On* (McClelland & Stewart: 1997) and *A Map to the Door of No Return* (Doubleday: 2001).

"Ghazal for Muzzles" quotes from "Zoo Station" on U2's *Achtung Baby* (Island: 1991).

"Ghazal for Bang Krut" is partly based on a small town on the Gulf of Thailand. Thanks to Emma and Allen.

"Ghazal for Gazelles" and "Ghazal For Once in A Lifetime, II" are what Agha Shahid Ali calls "real" ghazals. The former borrows from "Jesus Loves You," Margaret Atwood's poem, "Dream 2: Brian the Still-Hunter" (in *The Journals of Susanna Moodie*; Oxford: 1970), The Tragically Hip's "At the Hundredth Meridian" (on *Fully Completely*; MCA: 1992), and Margaret Avison's "The Swimmer's Moment" (from *Winter Sun*; UTP: 1962).

Various ghazals borrow lyrics from The Clash, including lines from "London Calling" in "Ghazal for June 4, 1989 (Failed)" and "Lost in the Supermarket" in "Ghazal for Empty Nets," both from *London Calling* (CBS/Epic: 1979) and "Rock the Casbah," from *Combat Rock* (CBS/Epic: 1982) in "Ghazal for Once in a Lifetime, I."

"Ghazal for S-21 (Failed)" refers to the infamous prison, now converted into the Teol Sleng Genocide Museum in Phnom Penh. "Preah Khan," in the same poem, is a disintegrating temple being overtaken by jungle at the Angkor Wat complex near Siam Reap. The poem partially quotes two titles: Spalding Gray's *Swimming to Cambodia* (Theatre Communications: 1985) and the Dead Kennedys single "Holiday in Cambodia" (Cherry Red: 1980).

"Ghazal for December 9, 1964" refers to albums and tracks by John Coltrane.

Various lines from "Ghazal for Once in a Lifetime" and "Ghazal for Once in a Lifetime, II" come from the Talking Heads song on *Remain in Light* (Sire Records: 1980). The names in the fourth couplet of "Ghazal for Once in a Lifetime, II" come from Mark Twain's *Adventures of Huckleberry Finn* (Chattos & Windus: 1884).

Acknowledgements

Hearty thanks to the Ontario Arts Council and the City of Ottawa for making this project possible.

Thanks also to Elizabeth Bachinsky at *Event* and rob mclennan's above/ground press for publishing previous versions of some of these poems, and to both John K. Samson and Kevin Connolly for spending careful time with the manuscript.

Thanks to Phyllis Webb for recalling her old kitchen nook, to Peter Sanger, Harry Thurston, Allan Cooper, Amanda Jernigan and Jana Graham for re-tuning *Stilt Jack*, and to Michael Ondaatje for introducing me to the work of Agha Shahid Ali.

Thanks to the folks at Arc and Carleton University for their interests in and promotion of the ghazal's history in North America and elsewhere.

For her editorial acuity and willingness to tell it like it is, with verve, I owe a great debt to Anita Lahey. For similar insights and red ink along the way, big thanks are also due to Matthew Holmes and Triny Finlay. For faith in the project and insight into its structural steel, thanks to Silas White and the rest of the crew at Nightwood, and to Carleton Wilson for his inspired book design.

Thanks, as always, are due to my family for their various forms of support.

And finally, for the home fires, the kindling, and all the love and patience, thanks are especially due to Kristal and Davis:

ground, counterweight, flight.

About the Author

Rob Winger grew up country in small-town Ontario before graduating to post-punk and new wave. His first book, *Muybridge's Horse*, was named a *Globe and Mail* Best Book for 2007, and was shortlisted for the Governor General's Award, Ottawa Book Award and Trillium Book Award for Poetry. An active editor and teacher, Rob recently completed a PhD in literature and cultural studies in Ottawa. He and his family live in the folk-rock hills northwest of Toronto.

PHOTO: Kristal Davis